COMPOSER
SHOWCASE
HAL LEONARD
STUDENT PIANO LIBRARY

T0210356

Magnificent OVERTURES

9 MOTIVATIONAL PIANO SOLOS
BY DENNIS ALEXANDER

ISBN 978-1-70514-329-2

Visit Hal Leonard Online at
www.halleonard.com

Contact us:
Hal Leonard
7777 West Bluemound Road
Milwaukee, WI 53213
Email: info@halleonard.com

In Europe, contact:
Hal Leonard Europe Limited
42 Wigmore Street
Marylebone, London, W1U 2RN
Email: info@halleonardeurope.com

In Australia, contact:
Hal Leonard Australia Pty. Ltd.
4 Lentara Court
Cheltenham, Victoria, 3192 Australia
Email: info@halleonard.com.au

Performance Notes

Capriccio in E Minor

This energetic piece is a great study for rapid alternating hands, while strengthening both hands via open fifths and blocked triads. It's important to *feel* this piece in cut time, with accents on beats one and two, which will help to propel the energy forward. The middle section also provides an opportunity to bring out the LH melody line over lighter accompanying notes in the RH.

Valse sentimentale

Students will need to achieve a warm, singing legato in this charming, lyrical waltz. Listen carefully to the dotted quarter notes, and match the dynamics to the succeeding eighth notes to avoid unwanted accents in that melodic line. This would also be a good opportunity to study the inflections of tasteful rubato.

Serenity

The harmonies within this piece should evoke gentle, rippling currents of flowing water. It's an excellent opportunity to work on relaxation and elegant choreography, floating out of the ends of those phrases in the RH that end with a half note.

Whimsy!

This sparkling, mischievous work is great fun to practice and perform! It's a terrific study for the LH in the middle section, and adherence to the fingering patterns will provide the confidence necessary to allow this hand to really shine.

Boundless Joy

Students will discover "boundless" opportunities for developing various technical skills in this spirited piece. Broken triads, LH over RH, hand contractions, scale patterns, chromatic runs, chord inversion—it's ALL here!

Scherzo Chromatique

Sparkling articulations, chromatic patterns, alternating hands, and lots of mixed meters all combine to create this humorous and playful solo. Be sure to exaggerate the dynamics, especially the softer sounds, to help create the energy and character that will make this such an effective solo!

Gardens in the Mist

Most students love these impressionistic sounds and colors, and this solo is full of whole-tone patterns and interesting harmonic colors. Beginning in m.13, play the RH sixteenth notes more on the pads of the fingers, keeping the sound very much in the distance, while the LH projects that legato, melodic line.

Mystical Odyssey

Imagine journeying through the Nile River and reveling in the wonders of the pyramids while performing this most colorful and expressive solo. The waters sometime flow rather rapidly in that middle section, so work to maintain even and "rippling" sixteenths between the hands.

Juxtaposition

If you're looking for an exciting showstopper, this will be the perfect candidate! "Juxtaposition" is defined as "the fact of two things being seen or placed close together with contrasting effect." The opening fifths of this solo are a perfect example of this, and the energy is enhanced by the opposing accents in each hand. Mixed meters add to the drama, in addition to the sweeping, spirited first and second inversion chords in the RH. A spirited tempo with great dynamic changes will tempt audiences to shout "Bravo"!

Preface

The word *overture* has been defined as "an introduction to something more substantial."
My Overture series for piano solo is just that!

Magnificent Overtures is the third book, and you'll find a mix of pieces that will motivate
and inspire. They are perfect for auditions, festivals, or recitals. Mixed meters, Lydian mode,
Impressionistic, Romantic, Contemporary, Boogie Woogie—it's all here. Each piece contains
technical and musical challenges, from lyrical melodic styles to fast rhythmical pieces.
There is something for everyone.

Enjoy these pieces, and may they be an introduction to more substantial works in your
musical journey!

Dennis Alexander
August 2021

Contents

Capriccio in E Minor

Dennis Alexander

Valse sentimentale

Dennis Alexander

Moderato (♩ = c. 116)

Serenity

Dennis Alexander

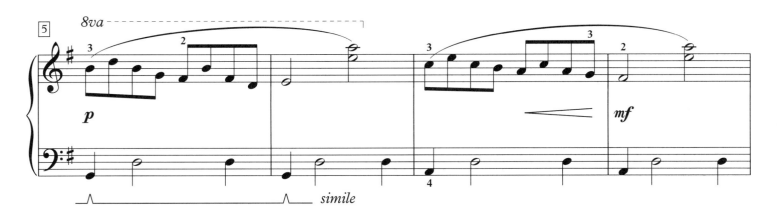

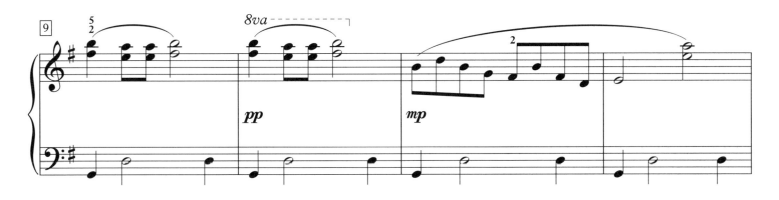

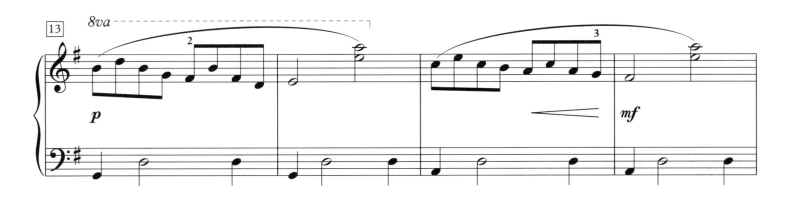

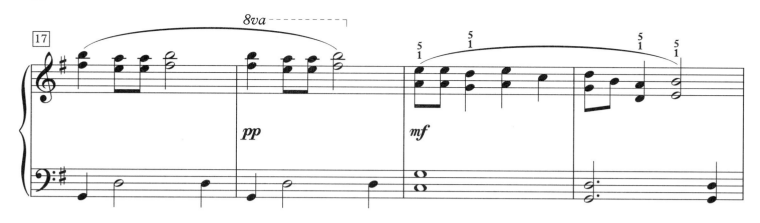

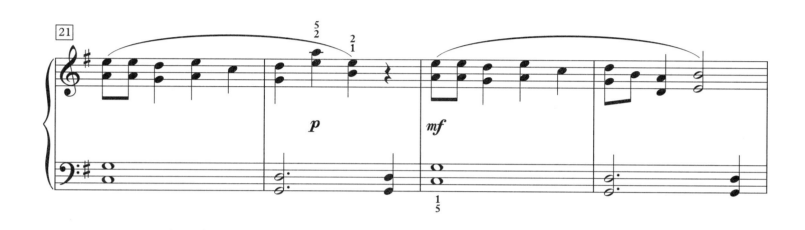

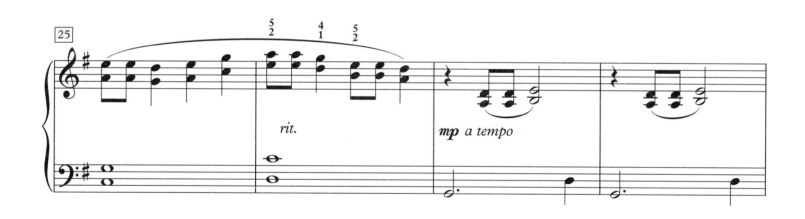

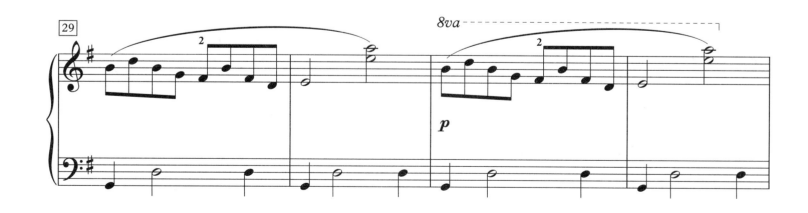

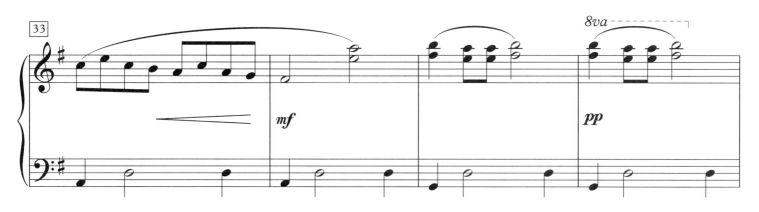

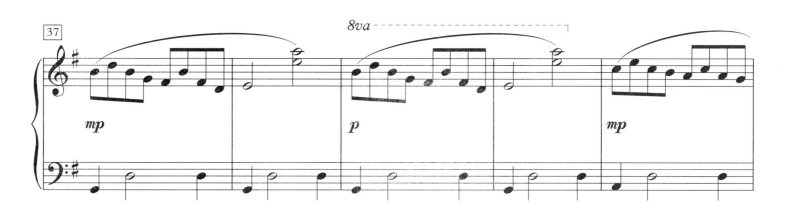

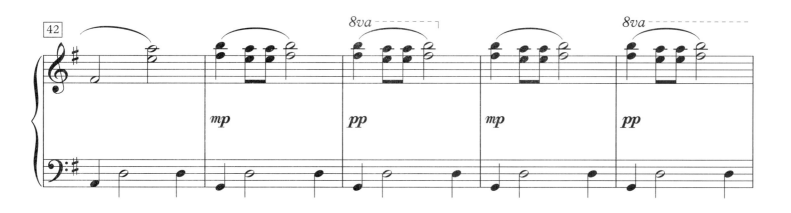

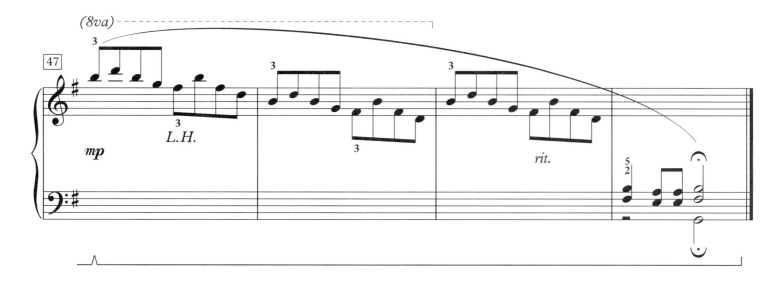

Whimsy!

Dennis Alexander

Boundless Joy

Dennis Alexander

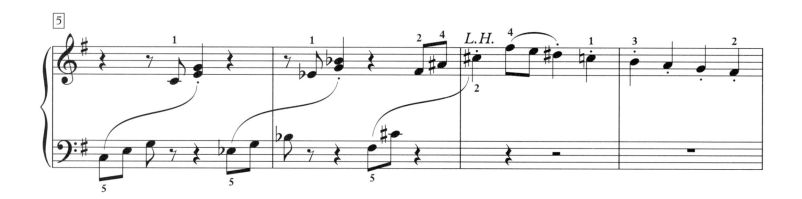

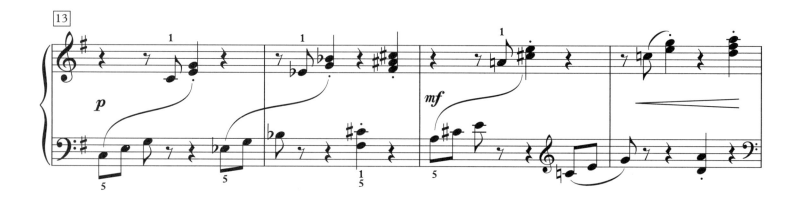

Scherzo Chromatique

Dennis Alexander

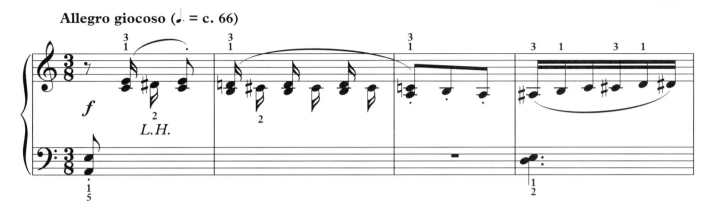

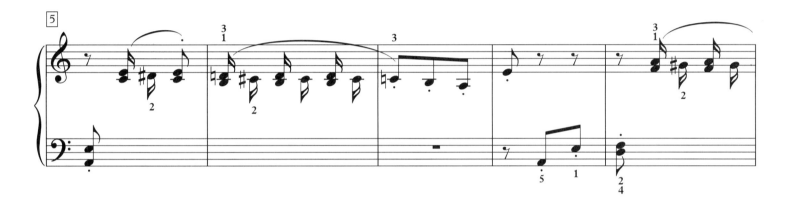

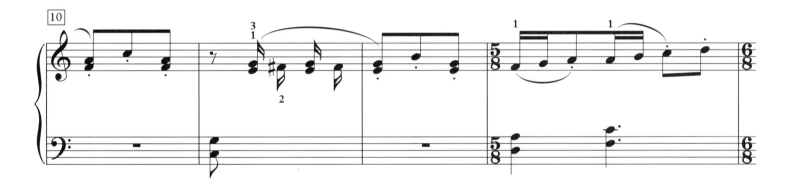

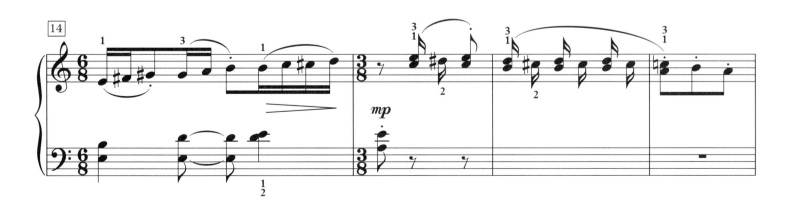

Gardens in the Mist

Dennis Alexander

Mystical Odyssey

Dennis Alexander

Juxtaposition

Dennis Alexander

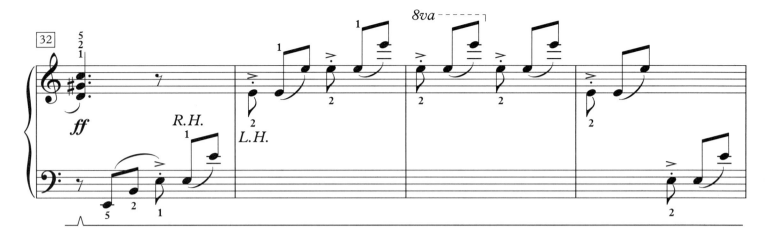

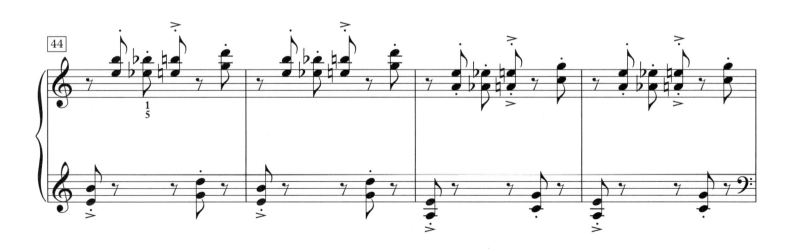

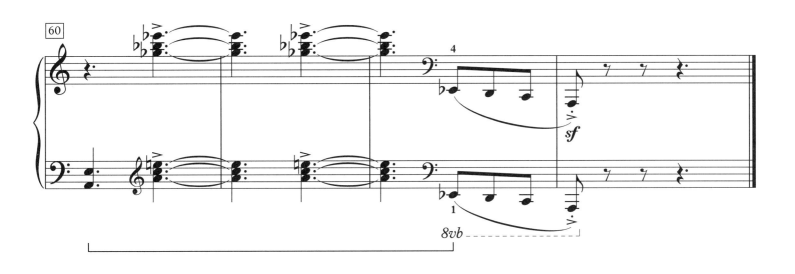

This series showcases great original piano music from our **Hal Leonard Student Piano Library** family of composers. Carefully graded for easy selection.

BILL BOYD

JAZZ BITS (AND PIECES)
Early Intermediate Level
00290312 11 Solos......................$7.99

JAZZ DELIGHTS
Intermediate Level
00240435 11 Solos......................$8.99

JAZZ FEST
Intermediate Level
00240436 10 Solos......................$8.99

JAZZ PRELIMS
Early Elementary Level
00290032 12 Solos......................$7.99

JAZZ SKETCHES
Intermediate Level
00220001 8 Solos......................$8.99

JAZZ STARTERS
Elementary Level
00290425 10 Solos......................$8.99

JAZZ STARTERS II
Late Elementary Level
00290434 11 Solos......................$7.99

JAZZ STARTERS III
Late Elementary Level
00290465 12 Solos......................$8.99

THINK JAZZ!
Early Intermediate Level
00290417 Method Book...........$12.99

TONY CARAMIA

JAZZ MOODS
Intermediate Level
00296728 8 Solos......................$6.95

SUITE DREAMS
Intermediate Level
00296775 4 Solos......................$6.99

SONDRA CLARK

DAKOTA DAYS
Intermediate Level
00296521 5 Solos......................$6.95

FLORIDA FANTASY SUITE
Intermediate Level
00296766 3 Duets......................$7.95

THREE ODD METERS
Intermediate Level
00296472 3 Duets......................$6.95

MATTHEW EDWARDS

CONCERTO FOR YOUNG PIANISTS
FOR 2 PIANOS, FOUR HANDS
Intermediate Level Book/CD
00296356 3 Movements $19.99

CONCERTO NO. 2 IN G MAJOR
FOR 2 PIANOS, 4 HANDS
Intermediate Level Book/CD
00296670 3 Movements............$17.99

PHILLIP KEVEREN

MOUSE ON A MIRROR
Late Elementary Level
00296361 5 Solos......................$8.99

MUSICAL MOODS
Elementary/Late Elementary Level
00296714 7 Solos......................$6.99

SHIFTY-EYED BLUES
Late Elementary Level
00296374 5 Solos......................$7.99

CAROL KLOSE

THE BEST OF CAROL KLOSE
Early to Late Intermediate Level
00146151 15 Solos...................$12.99

CORAL REEF SUITE
Late Elementary Level
00296354 7 Solos......................$7.50

DESERT SUITE
Intermediate Level
00296667 6 Solos......................$7.99

FANCIFUL WALTZES
Early Intermediate Level
00296473 5 Solos......................$7.95

GARDEN TREASURES
Late Intermediate Level
00296787 5 Solos......................$8.50

ROMANTIC EXPRESSIONS
Intermediate to Late Intermediate Level
00296923 5 Solos......................$8.99

WATERCOLOR MINIATURES
Early Intermediate Level
00296848 7 Solos......................$7.99

JENNIFER LINN

AMERICAN IMPRESSIONS
Intermediate Level
00296471 6 Solos......................$8.99

ANIMALS HAVE FEELINGS TOO
Early Elementary/Elementary Level
00147789 8 Solos......................$8.99

AU CHOCOLAT
Late Elementary/Early Intermediate Level
00298110 7 Solos......................$8.99

CHRISTMAS IMPRESSIONS
Intermediate Level
00296706 8 Solos......................$8.99

JUST PINK
Elementary Level
00296722 9 Solos......................$8.99

LES PETITES IMAGES
Late Elementary Level
00296664 7 Solos......................$8.99

LES PETITES IMPRESSIONS
Intermediate Level
00296355 6 Solos......................$8.99

REFLECTIONS
Late Intermediate Level
00296843 5 Solos......................$8.99

TALES OF MYSTERY
Intermediate Level
00296769 6 Solos......................$8.99

LYNDA LYBECK-ROBINSON

ALASKA SKETCHES
Early Intermediate Level
00119637 8 Solos......................$8.99

AN AWESOME ADVENTURE
Late Elementary Level
00137563 8 Solos......................$7.99

FOR THE BIRDS
Early Intermediate/Intermediate Level
00237078 9 Solos......................$8.99

WHISPERING WOODS
Late Elementary Level
00275905 9 Solos......................$8.99

MONA REJINO

CIRCUS SUITE
Late Elementary Level
00296665 5 Solos......................$8.99

COLOR WHEEL
Early Intermediate Level
00201951 6 Solos......................$9.99

IMPRESIONES DE ESPAÑA
Intermediate Level
00337520 6 Solos......................$8.99

IMPRESSIONS OF NEW YORK
Intermediate Level
00364212......................$8.99

JUST FOR KIDS
Elementary Level
00296840 8 Solos......................$7.99

MERRY CHRISTMAS MEDLEYS
Intermediate Level
00296799 5 Solos......................$8.99

MINIATURES IN STYLE
Intermediate Level
00148088 6 Solos......................$8.99

PORTRAITS IN STYLE
Early Intermediate Level
00296507 6 Solos......................$8.99

EUGÉNIE ROCHEROLLE

CELEBRATION SUITE
Intermediate Level
00152724 3 Duets......................$8.99

**ENCANTOS ESPAÑOLES
(SPANISH DELIGHTS)**
Intermediate Level
00125451 6 Solos......................$8.99

JAMBALAYA
Intermediate Level
00296654 2 Pianos, 8 Hands.....$12.99
00296725 2 Pianos, 4 Hands.......$7.95

JEROME KERN CLASSICS
Intermediate Level
00296577 10 Solos...................$12.99

LITTLE BLUES CONCERTO
Early Intermediate Level
00142801 2 Pianos, 4 Hands......$12.99

TOUR FOR TWO
Late Elementary Level
00296832 6 Duets......................$9.99

TREASURES
Late Elementary/Early Intermediate Level
00296924 7 Solos......................$8.99

JEREMY SISKIND

BIG APPLE JAZZ
Intermediate Level
00278209 8 Solos......................$8.99

MYTHS AND MONSTERS
Late Elementary/Early Intermediate Level
00148148 9 Solos......................$8.99

CHRISTOS TSITSAROS

DANCES FROM AROUND THE WORLD
Early Intermediate Level
00296688 7 Solos......................$8.99

FIVE SUMMER PIECES
Late Intermediate/Advanced Level
00361235 5 Solos......................$12.99

LYRIC BALLADS
Intermediate/Late Intermediate Level
00102404 6 Solos......................$8.99

POETIC MOMENTS
Intermediate Level
00296403 8 Solos......................$8.99

SEA DIARY
Early Intermediate Level
00253486 9 Solos......................$8.99

SONATINA HUMORESQUE
Late Intermediate Level
00296772 3 Movements..............$6.99

SONGS WITHOUT WORDS
Intermediate Level
00296506 9 Solos......................$9.99

THREE PRELUDES
Early Advanced Level
00130747 3 Solos......................$8.99

THROUGHOUT THE YEAR
Late Elementary Level
00296723 12 Duets......................$6.95

ADDITIONAL COLLECTIONS

AT THE LAKE
by Elvina Pearce
Elementary/Late Elementary Level
00131642 10 Solos and Duets.....$7.99

CHRISTMAS FOR TWO
by Dan Fox
Early Intermediate Level
00290069 13 Duets....................$8.99

CHRISTMAS JAZZ
by Mike Springer
Intermediate Level
00296525 6 Solos......................$8.99

COUNTY RAGTIME FESTIVAL
by Fred Kern
Intermediate Level
00296882 7 Solos......................$7.99

LITTLE JAZZERS
by Jennifer Watts
Elementary/Late Elementary Level
00154573 9 Solos......................$8.99

PLAY THE BLUES!
by Luann Carman
Early Intermediate Level
00296357 10 Solos......................$9.99

ROLLER COASTERS & RIDES
by Jennifer & Mike Watts
Intermediate Level
00131144 8 Duets......................$8.99

HAL•LEONARD®
www.halleonard.com

Prices, contents, and availability subject
to change without notice.